Dark Psychology and Manipulation

Influencing People Using NLP and Mind Control. Learn about Hypnosis, Emotional Intelligence, and Brainwashing through body language (2022 Guide for Beginners)

Fred Field

CONTENTS

INTRODUCTION

Dark psychology is the study of how we intentionally harm those around us. People who instinctively manipulate others typically follow very specific patterns that they use to control others. These behavioural patterns are so predictable that they have been identified as a predictor of dark behaviour. Dark personalities, such as those of sociopaths, narcissists, and Machiavellians, are naturally manipulative. We can learn about how people think and what makes their minds tick. We can learn how people can be influenced, and we can also learn how to influence people for the better by studying and learning from these people.

This series has been meticulously crafted to educate you to step by step, with each book building on the previous. You will be given a step-by-step guide to everything from mastering the art of manipulation to becoming a powerful hypnotist capable of hypnotizing your friends, family, and strangers.

Though this may appear to be a small book, rest assured that we have condensed all of the information you require to truly manifest your most powerful self.

Within these books, you will begin to get a taste of exactly this; you will begin to learn about dark psychology and manipulation.

You will learn everything there is to know about manipulation, how it works, and why it works the way it does, as well as the signs to look for if someone else is attempting to manipulate you. This is critical information for you—you must be aware of what is going on to protect yourself.

This book will teach you why we are so vulnerable to dark psychology, delving into the fact that, ultimately, the way people's minds work leaves them vulnerable. You will learn how to recognize red flags and the effects of manipulation. This will assist you in identifying several common tactics used by manipulators. You will also learn how to take control of those tactics.

We'll look at neuro-linguistic programming, a type of subtle influencing technique that allows you to change someone else's mind, encouraging them to do whatever you want by learning to communicate with their subconscious minds instead, completely bypassing conscious detection, and we'll apply this to hypnosis as well.

I've added a closing chapter in each book that introduces you to the next book to make this series easier to use and navigate.

Please have fun.

CHAPTER 1
WILL BE A PATH IN THE DARK PSYCHOLOGY TO PENETRATE AND DWELL IN ALL THAT CONCERNS THE MANIPULATION?

What Exactly Is Dark Psychology?

Dark psychology functions as a tool. All tools can be used to create new things or to destroy existing ones. While we will discuss dark psychology and how it has been used against you, this is not a how-to guide for you to do the same. It is a method for recognizing and defending against it, as well as twisting it for personal benefit. You can better defend yourself against dark psychology if you understand what it is.

Consider how you might see manipulation in the media or with politicians. They can manipulate you for either good or evil. It is entirely up to you to decide how you will employ it.

The brain is without a doubt the most complicated organ in the human body. It has intricate mechanisms that make it complex and difficult to comprehend. We still don't fully comprehend why it works the way it does.

We do have a little insight that can help us better understand ourselves and others. If you are unaware of the basic machinery of your brain, you may be putting yourself at risk of being converted by others.

The less we understand about our brains and emotions, the more vulnerable we are to allowing others to take advantage of this complex organ.

Within our brains, we have an incredible amount of power.

We can remember things, generate new ideas, and solve our life's most difficult problems all within the same organ.

We can, however, use the power of these same mechanisms to manipulate others, brainwash them into believing something that isn't true, and persuade them to do terrible things.

The only thing we know about our brains is what we've learned about them! The only way we can interact with other people is by controlling these complex devices.

You won't be able to get a new transplant from another person for a different brain, and once your brain is damaged, it's extremely difficult to repair depending on the part that was injured.

One thing we should remember about our brains is that they are always malleable. Just because you were born with a certain brain doesn't mean you'll have it for the rest of your life.

You can rewire your brain. This is crucial for understanding your psychology. However, when we start talking about dark psychology, things get a little more complicated.

Dark psychology refers to how we can manipulate our brains to get what other people want from us.

When we talk about psychology, we're talking about how you interact with the world. Your basic psychology is comprised of what motivates you, what causes you pain, what drives you, what you enjoy, what you dislike, and so on.

When you have problems with your brain, such as depression or anxiety, you can see a psychologist who will help you diagnose yourself based on your symptoms.

Dark psychology is something that is less discussed in the professional world, but it is important to understand in our daily lives.

This is because someone is attempting to persuade us at all times of the day and night. Persuasive tactics could be used against you, whether it's a toxic boyfriend or a commercial that plays in between episodes of your favourite show.

Humans have amazing minds, which means that if you can control more than one mind, you can wield more power.

Who Is Using Dark Psychology Nowadays?

Narcissists

People who are clinically diagnosed as narcissistic have an extremely inflated sense of self-worth. They require a confirmation from others that they are superior. They've wished to be adored and respected. They use dark psychology, manipulation, and unethical persuasion to keep them.

Sociopaths

Genuinely sociopathic people (those who meet the clinical criteria) are frequently pleasant, talented, and significant. They employ dark tactics to establish a shallow relationship and then take advantage of people due to a lack of emotionality and the ability to feel guilt.

Attorneys

Many attorneys are so focused on winning their case that they resort to dark manipulation techniques to achieve the desired result.

Politicians

Many politicians use dark psychology and dark persuasion to persuade people that they are correct and win votes.

Salesmen

Many salespeople become so focused on making a sale that they resort to unethical tactics to motivate and persuade someone to buy their product.

Leaders

Many leaders employ shady tactics to elicit obedience from their subordinates. They employ these strategies to exert greater effort or achieve higher levels of performance.

Speakers in Public

Many speakers use dark strategies to increase the emotional state of the audience, knowing that it leads to more products being sold at the back of the room.

People who are self-centred

It could be someone who prioritizes their interests over the interests of others.

First, they will use tactics to satisfy their desires, even if it means harming someone else. They don't mind if they win or lose.

Traits of Dark Psychology

Narcissism

Narcissism is the dark trait that narcissists exhibit.

Grandiosity, superiority, dominance, and entitlement are all characteristics of narcissists. They are charming people with a positive attitude, which is why they are good at deceiving others.

Machiavellianism

Machiavellianism is a sinister trait characterized by deception and manipulation. Machiavellians are cynical people (not because they are sceptical or have a sceptical curiosity; they just don't like the moral constraints that the rest of society adheres to). They are typically amoral and self-interested. They don't have a sense of right and wrong; they'll do anything as long as it's in their best interests.

Machiavellians are cold, unprincipled people who excel at interpersonal manipulation. They believe that life is a zero-sum game and that manipulating others is the key to success. They approach all types of relationships with a cold, calculated attitude, and when they want a specific outcome in a given situation, the end always justifies the means.

Psychopathy
Psychopathy is the most malevolent of all the dark traits.

Because psychopaths lack empathy, they are unconcerned about others. They, on the other hand, have extremely high levels of impulsiveness and are thrill-seekers. They are callous, manipulative, and have an exaggerated sense of grandeur. They seek thrills without regard for the harm they cause to others in the process.

Psychopaths are harder to detect than you might think. They tend to maintain normal outward appearances; despite their lack of empathy and conscience, they learn to act normally by observing the emotional reactions of others. When they are attempting to manipulate you, they can even appear charming. They are erratic and have criminal tendencies, though this is not always the case.

CHAPTER 2
WHERE DO WE FIND DARK PSYCHOLOGY AND MANIPULATION IN LIFE?

Manipulation Detection and Avoidance

Now that we know a little bit more about manipulation and what it entails, we must also learn how to spot manipulation. We all have wants and needs that we try to meet, but most of us will follow a code of ethics and the law to help us decide whether or not to pursue those things. The manipulator, on the other hand, is unconcerned about the rules and laws, and they will happily influence someone, often in a covert manner, using deceptive or abusive tactics to get what they want.

Of course, the target will be unaware of what the manipulator is up to. If they do, the manipulator will be exposed, and they will never be able to get their target to listen again, and the manipulator will lose control. They have to be covert about the actions they use or they will lose out—which is why it is difficult to recognize when you are being manipulated.

Because each person is unique, the manipulator employs a variety of techniques, and the ones they employ on you will be determined by the analysis they were able to obtain on you. They will frequently rely on friendliness and niceness to persuade you to trust them. Often, there will be an excessive amount of flattery involved to get their target to open up and talk with the manipulator. Even if they do not understand empathy, the manipulator knows how to make the other person in the relationship feel special and important, but they are doing so to achieve their own end goal.

The manipulator may not use much flattery. To get what they want out of the target, the manipulator may become abusive and hostile at times, especially as the relationship progresses. When a manipulator chooses this path, the object with that person is to see how much power they can gain, though other factors may also be at play. In some cases, the manipulator is so skilled at using hostility and other techniques that the target is unaware of what is going on.

Some manipulators deny making certain promises, reaching certain agreements, or even have ever had a conversation. They will even blame their victim for something the victim did not do to gain power or sympathy.

This method is used to get out of a contract, promise, or deadline. You may even witness a form of manipulation with parents who like to bribe their children, such as "finish your dinner to get dessert."

Another thing to keep an eye out for with manipulation is that the manipulator frequently makes assumptions about your beliefs and intentions, and then reacts to them as if they were true. This is one of the ways they can rationalize their actions or feelings. Simultaneously, they will continue to deny what the victim said during the conversation. The manipulator may act as if something has been decided or agreed upon when it has not, to silence any objections you may have about the situation.

The foot in the door technique is another technique that the manipulator may want to try. This is a popular technique, so be cautious if you suspect someone is attempting to use it against you. When we see this type of technique, we notice that the manipulator begins with a small request, one that isn't too big of a deal, and one that they are fairly certain their target will agree to help with. When the target agrees to assist with the smaller request, the manipulator will immediately follow up with their larger request. This second request will be much more demanding and larger. However, because the victim agreed to assist in the first instance, they feel obligated to do so again.

The victim believes they still have a choice because they can say no. However, if they refuse the second request, the manipulator will have the upper hand. They can act offended by the denial and turn the victim's words around to ensure that the manipulator is the one who is offended in all of this. Remember that the manipulator is skilled at making any situation about themselves and their complaints, regardless of how much they are harming or inconveniencing the target.

You may also notice that feigning concern is another technique that a manipulator tries and employs on their target to obtain what they desire. This one is frequently successful with the manipulator because it helps to undermine the target's confidence as well as the decisions he or she makes. After all, the manipulator can hide in worry and warnings about the victim by using fake concerns. Others may interpret it as a compliment or that the manipulator is genuinely concerned, but to someone who knows them better, it is essentially a veiled threat if the target does what they want.

When you come into contact with a manipulator in your life and are unsure how to react or how to avoid being taken advantage of, the best advice is to be cautious. The manipulator will try to sneak in under your radar, and if you are not paying attention, they will most likely get in and cause significant damage without your knowledge.

First, observe how they behave in your presence. Do they seem to lavish you with compliments although they don't know you? And have you noticed that the flattery appears to be superficial and unrelated to anything you have done in particular? Do you notice that they ask a lot of questions to keep you talking, but when you try to delve deeper and learn more about them, they become defensive and angry, only offering one-word answers? Do you feel guilty, sad, or depressed when you're around this person?

You may have a manipulator on your hands depending on how you answer these questions. Being aware of and on the lookout for any of the tricks and techniques discussed earlier in this section can help you avoid the manipulator and ensure that they do not gain power over you.

How to Recognize a Fellow Manipulator

While manipulating others may be beneficial to you, being manipulated by another is not. As a result, knowing how to spot a manipulator is just as important as knowing how to manipulate.

Some people are simply born manipulators endowed with the gift of gab, and these natural-born manipulators all appear to share some common characteristics, as described by psychiatrist Abigail Brenner:

- They are not capable of genuine altruism. Manipulative people rarely, if ever, do something out of the goodness of their hearts; there is always an ulterior motive.

- They're good talkers, but that's about it. Manipulators rarely follow up grandiose speeches or ideas with actual action. They build these incredible castles in the sky to entice you, with no intention of ever following through on any commitments or promises they may make.

- They have no empathy. Manipulators either refuse to empathize with others or are incapable of doing so. You might notice a manipulator in this manner, for example, if your company is downsizing.

- They are superior gossipers to the average high school girl.

- Manipulators enjoy making people squirm, and what better way to do so than by spreading malicious stories or publicizing the mistakes of others? Your coworker who is standing at the water cooler telling everyone about Sarah's divorce and revelling in the gory details may be a manipulator.

- They will take advantage of any kindness you show them. Manipulators will take a mile if you give them an inch.

- Manipulators take advantage of people; it's what they do—and there's no easier way for them to do so than if you've already opened the door for them to abuse you by doing them a favour or being nice to them.

- They enjoy pointing fingers. Manipulators do not want to accept responsibility for their wrongdoings, so they try to blame someone else—even if it means destroying that person's career, relationships, or friendships.

- They have no boundaries. Manipulators typically do not understand or care about the social contract that governs the rules of etiquette to which the rest of us adhere. A manipulator may ask you questions that are a little too personal, may call you about a work-related matter at an unreasonable hour, or may unexpectedly show up at your house. They don't understand or care about the concept of "rudeness."

- They are unwilling to make a concession. It's either their way or the highway for them.

- Manipulators demand that things be done exactly the way they want them to be done. It is unknown whether this is due to a desire to assert authority or an inborn defect.

Of course, the psychopath is another "natural-born" manipulator that must be identified. Psychopaths share five characteristics, according to Amy Morin, psychotherapist and author of *13 Things Mentally Strong People Do Not Do:*

1. They believe they are significant. This is crucial. Psychopaths have a colossal sense of self and frequently believe they are the centre of the universe. Psychopaths frequently demand special or superior treatment as a result of their inflated egos.

2. They cannot feel guilt or remorse. Psychopaths have no conscience. They can think about things that would make others gag in disgust.

3. They are masters of deception. You can refer back to the common characteristics of manipulators listed above in this case. Psychopaths are extremely skilled at guilt-tripping others, as well as flattery and seduction. Because of their ability to manipulate, you may find yourself unknowingly or unwittingly obeying a psychopath's every command.

4. They are extremely endearing. This falls under the category of flattery and seduction mentioned earlier. Psychopaths are excellent at persuading others to join their "team." They smile and joke their way into the lives of those around them, and these people are frequently unable to recognize the psychopath for what he or she is.

5. They are also extremely ruthless. You'll know if you've crossed a psychopath because they'll likely retaliate with small (or large) acts of vengeance.

But how do you spot a psychopath in the crowd? Prakash Masand, the founder of the Centers of Psychiatric Excellence, believes the following signs indicate a psychopath:

- They are irresponsible and have no regard for other people's safety. The Wall Street bankers who threw the United States into an economic crisis in 2008 as a result of shady hedge fund trading with derivatives are a prime example of this. Many of them were well aware that they would be driving others into bankruptcy, but they went ahead and did it anyway for their benefit.

- They infringe on the rights of others. As an example, consider the case of Robert Maxwell, the obscenely wealthy publishing magnate who was discovered after his death to have stolen millions by defrauding the pension funds of thousands of innocent people.

- They engage in socially irresponsible behaviour such as binge drinking, narcotic addiction, promiscuous sexual behaviour, or other criminal activities. Ted Bundy, the infamous serial killer and promising law student who confessed to murdering 30 women in his spare time, is an example of a psychopath engaging in socially irresponsible (or rather, reprehensible) behaviour.

- They frequently run afoul of the law. This is a natural result of irresponsible social behaviour and violating the rights of others. Psychopaths are not always caught red-handed for murder; sometimes their transgressions are as minor as failing to recognize that the speed limit applies to them, resulting in a small mountain of fines.

- They enjoy inflicting pain on others and are frequently sadists. Ilse Koch, the wife of a Nazi secret service member, was an example of this. She would walk around naked in a Jewish concentration camp and have any man who even dared to look at her shot on the spot.

- An inability or apathy toward distinguishing between right and wrong. Psychopaths are either unconcerned about doing the right thing or are unaware that they are doing the wrong thing. The "angel of mercy" stereotype, which can be found in the study of criminology, is an example of this. Offenders who fit this stereotype murder in the mistaken belief that by euthanizing the victim, they are doing the victim a favour.

- The proclivity to lie. Often. Quite frequently. Because psychopaths lack a moral compass, they have no reason to be truthful if it does not benefit them in some way. They have no qualms about fabricating stories about themselves, whether for sympathy or adoration.

Manipulation Examples

There are numerous real-life examples of manipulation occurring right in front of you daily. If you look closely, you might notice how certain people use manipulation and blackmail to get their way in life. Such incidents are common in the workplace. When there is something valuable at stake in a family situation, manipulation takes place. For example, if a wealthy person dies without leaving a clear will, many people will fight to gain control of the deceased's assets.

The case of Jonestown is a real-life example of manipulation (Guyana). The Jonestown story is one of the most well-documented examples of manipulation and brainwashing. Jim Jones, a religious/cult leader, was the mastermind behind the story.

During the early 1970s, Jim Jones rose to prominence in Northwest Guyana.

His meteoric rise to fame was linked to supernatural occurrences. Jones, like all manipulative people, was able to gather a small group of brainwashed people around him.

Isolation is one of the key characteristics of manipulative

people, as previously stated. Manipulators who want to gain public influence and control large crowds, on the other hand, do not rely solely on isolation. The inner-circle approach is used by the majority of public manipulators. An inner circle is made up of people who believe in the manipulator's ideologies. The ideologies are frequently regarded as correct, and nothing is seen to be wrong with them. This is the approach taken by the majority of cultic sects. When a person is introduced to the inner circle, they are made to feel special, but they are also required to fulfil certain conditions. In most cases, members of the inner circle are required to swear allegiance to the sect's leader.

Jim Jones, like all sects, began by forming a small circle of people who would later work as recruiters. Jonestown's entire village began to subscribe to Jones' ideologies and teachings. After a while, many people agreed with his teachings. The social pressure associated with sect members drew even more people in. The more people who joined the sect, the more cunning the man became. In the mid-1970s, Jim Jones declared himself to be a god who had come to save the people from their plight. Given that the case occurred during a period when people were experiencing economic hardship, the leader took advantage of the situation. The poor villagers were drawn to him in the hope that he would improve their lot in life.

They gave him their undivided attention and allowed him to take control of their entire lives.

Jim Jones, like all manipulative leaders, was unconcerned about the welfare of the people. He did not deliver on his promises.

Instead, he took advantage of his celebrity to amass wealth from the victims. He enticed the victims into giving him sexual favours and eventually gained control of the entire village.

The story of Jim Jones culminated in the massacre of over 900 followers of the sect leader. The town was named after this merciless sect leader who didn't care about the people's well-being. He didn't mind killing 900 people to get what he wanted because he was a manipulative person. Although the Jonestown story is an extreme case in which a person exhibited sociopathic tendencies, it reveals the true character of a manipulative person. Most manipulators are unconcerned about how you feel or think. They want to make money and move on with their lives.

How to Handle Manipulation

There is no doubt that you will encounter manipulative people in your life. In your pursuit of success, you will come across people who want to use your money or ride on your back. Those people will use a variety of manipulative techniques to try to take control of your life. You must find a way to keep them under control. Controlling manipulative people entails preventing them from starting in the first place. The following are some strategies for dealing with manipulative people:

- **Maintain your vigilance**: If you are aware that you are a target, you must remain vigilant at all times. In other words, we must all remain vigilant. People will come to you to take advantage of your situation because everyone is a prime target for manipulation. Being observant means being able to read people's intentions by looking at them.

- **Be secretive:** Don't be the person who tells everyone everything. A manipulative person can only exert control over you if they have information about you. If the manipulator has no information about you, they may not have any legitimate reasons to control your life.

- **Control your emotions by doing the following**: NLP practitioners do not require you to speak to gather information. NLP experts place a greater emphasis on the emotional cues you send out during conversations. You must learn to control both your expressive and physiological emotions.

- **Isolation should be avoided**: Try as hard as you can to avoid allowing a manipulative person to isolate you. When you are alone, you are vulnerable and weak. The majority of manipulative people gain power during times of weakness, such as isolation.

Manipulative Strategies to Avoid

If you've found yourself in the presence of someone who is controlling you or have a strong suspicion that they are, this is how you can alert them.

They Attempt to deceive

We all value honesty and accountability, but con artists either conceal the truth or attempt to show you only one side of the story. Consider the boss or employee who deliberately spreads unverified rumours and gossip to gain a tactical advantage.

Tactic: Don't believe everything you hear. Instead, base your decisions on well-known facts and pose questions when specifics are unclear.

They reap the benefits of your happiness.

When we're in a particularly good mood, we're prone to saying yes to anything or jumping on opportunities that seem great at the time (but we didn't think through the implications). Manipulators understand how to manipulate different moods.

Tactic: Attempt to make your positive feelings as conscious as your negative feelings. When making decisions, try to strike a balance.

Worry is a game they're playing.

A trickster will misrepresent facts and overemphasize specific points to frighten you into action.

Tactic: Be wary of comments that imply you lack courage or attempt to instil fear of falling out. Before you take any action, make sure you have a complete picture of the problem.

They are attempting to gain an advantage in the domestic court.

A deceptive person may insist on meeting and engaging in a physical space where more power and influence can be wielded.

These individuals may attempt to negotiate in an environment where they feel control and familiarity, such as their workplace, home, or another location where they may feel less secure.

If you need to talk, use this tactic to invite you to do so in a neutral setting. If you have to meet the individual on their property, ask for a drink and engage in small talk upon arrival to help you get your bearings.

They Take Advantage of Reciprocity

Manipulators understand that it is more difficult to say no if they do you a favour, so they may try to impress you, cheese you up, or say yes to small favours... and then ask for large ones.

Of course, offering brings more delight than receiving.

Knowing your limitations, on the other hand, is critical. And don't be afraid to say no if necessary.

The Exhibit Pessimistic Feelings

A few people purposefully raise their voices or use powerful body language to show they're angry in an attempt to control their feelings.

Timeout practice is a good tactic. Pause for a moment to respond if someone is displaying strong emotions. In some cases, you may also need to take a few moments to move away.

They ask a lot of questions.

It's easy to talk about ourselves. Manipulators are aware of this and take advantage of it by asking questions with a hidden agenda in the hopes of uncovering hidden vulnerabilities or knowledge that they can use to their advantage.

Tactic: Of course, you should not suspect false motives in anyone who wishes to effectively understand you. However, be wary of those who only ask questions while refusing to reveal the same information about themselves.

They provide you with an extremely limited amount of time to act.

Someone may try to compel you to decide in a very short period. By doing so, they attempt to persuade you to decide before you have even had a chance to consider the implications.

Don't give in to unreasonable demands. When your partner refuses to give you more time, you're better off going somewhere else to get what you need.

They Make an effort to speak quickly.

Manipulators frequently speak at a faster pace or use different terminology and phrases to gain an advantage.

Tactic: Do not be afraid to ask people to elaborate on their statements or to ask specific questions. You could also paraphrase their argument or ask them to provide an example, allowing you to reclaim control of the narrative.

They're Using the Silent Treatment on You

By purposefully failing to respond to your acceptable calls, texts, emails, or other inquiries, the manipulator assumes power and intends to create doubt and confusion in your mind.

The silent treatment is a power game in which secrecy is used as a weapon.

After you've tried some communication with your partner, set a time limit for them. In cases where solutions are not readily available, it may be appropriate to have an open discussion about their contact style.

CHAPTER 3
EXPLANATION OF MANIPULATION AND THE EFFECTS IT HAS ON PEOPLE

We're talking about psychological manipulation when we talk about the manipulation that doesn't involve using force or controlling someone's finances. Psychological manipulation is a type of social influence that influences a person's perception of the world or their behaviour through deceptive or covert means.

Manipulation is further subdivided into two categories: positive manipulation and negative manipulation. When someone is manipulated for their good, this is referred to as positive manipulation. A doctor attempting to persuade a patient to quit smoking is an example of this. Negative manipulation is the opposite of positive manipulation in that it involves manipulating another person for ulterior motives or personal gain. A salesman attempting to persuade a customer to purchase a product that he knows is defective or will not be suitable for the buyer is an example of negative manipulation.

While people can negatively use manipulation, it is important to remember that manipulation can also be used positively. Because so many people perceive manipulation as a negative thing, they may fail to recognize how powerful a psychological art form of manipulation can be. Furthermore, many people fail to recognize that we all use manipulation in some form or another just by going about our daily lives. While we may not recognize this type of behaviour as manipulation right away, we will all have some experience with it.

Understanding that there is more to the art of manipulation than just the act of manipulation itself will help you understand what can help the process run more smoothly. While beginners may believe that they can do it without the persuasion and analysis aspects, you will quickly discover that the results aren't as good and that you are less likely to get what you want if these two parts are skipped.

Manipulation: How and Why Does It Work?

Assume for a moment that you don't already know the other person and haven't been able to gain their trust before attempting to manipulate them. As a result, whenever you ask the other person for something, they will simply say no.

Manipulation Error

How many times have you turned on the television and heard about some group or cult taking advantage of someone, or perhaps a smaller group of people, and convincing them to change their entire personalities and more? You may have heard about people who are willing to kill, attack, and do more despite being the calmest and most controlled person on the planet before this all happening.

This is a little extreme, but there are many instances when manipulation is viewed negatively. When this occurs, it is usually because the manipulator is looking to get what they want, to gain something, regardless of the consequences to the other person.

They may even want the target to become reliant on them so that they can return and use that person as often as they want.

In this situation, the target is frequently harmed or injured in some way.

Whether they are physically harmed as a result of the process, or they are simply led to believe that they aren't worth anything at all, it can be extremely damaging to the target. The manipulator is the only person who can benefit from this type of manipulation.

CHAPTER 4
DIFFERENT TYPES OF
MANIPULATION
TECHNIQUES

Brainwashing

Brainwashing is unique in that it has a method that has been codified. If you look closely, you will notice that brainwashing steps are used in many different areas of life and by many different organizations. Cults, government operations, businesses, advertising, news media, and a variety of other organizations use them. Brainwashing is accomplished through a series of steps. First, a person's sense of self is dismantled. A healthy, normal person has a sense of self that gives them identity and confidence. A person's sense of self is what allows them to function in the world without becoming overly persuaded or suggestible. The first step in brainwashing is to break this down to make the person more susceptible.

This can take many forms; for example, the person may be told that they are not valid or worthy of respect. It is possible that the individual is subjected to physical challenges and is not allowed to relax or take their time doing anything. It could be either verbal or physical. The breaking down of the self essentially serves to increase the person's likelihood of latching onto the ideas that the brainwasher wants them to believe. By destroying a person's sense of self, they no longer believe in themselves, but rather in the person doing the brainwashing. This is especially noticeable in the military.

Hypnosis

The next major application of dark persuasion that will be discussed is hypnosis. Hypnosis can happen with or without the individual's knowledge. If a person is aware that they are being hypnotized, they may be more aware of what is happening, but they are still vulnerable to manipulation.

Hypnosis is used for a variety of purposes, and it can be used to effect both positive and negative change. There are several elements to hypnosis, and they may or may not be present in different iterations of the hypnosis process. It all begins with an induction. Remember in cartoons when the swirling visual effect is depicted, and some head-wrapped mystic is holding a watch with the swirl in front of a person's face? This cartoon depicts what is formally known as the induction process.

Deception

The final major method of dark persuasion we'll discuss is deception. Deception is similar to lying, but it contains some distinct elements. One of them is ambiguity. When someone makes vague or ambiguous statements, this is referred to as equivocation. The goal is to make things unclear so that you can't point out the flaw in their logic. Deception is the act of making something appear to be something it is not. Deception occurs when a person employs any method to make a situation appear to be different than it is. One example is lying by omission. Lying by omission occurs when a person withholds important information to influence others' perceptions of reality. Deception occurs without a person's knowledge and alters their perception of the situation without actually lying. Another example of this deception technique is camouflage. This occurs when someone tries to conceal the truth in such a way that another person does not notice that they are missing some crucial details of the story. When someone uses half-truths, this will be used. Camouflage occurs when someone tries to conceal their true identity or what they do for a living. In metaphorical terms, camouflaging can be thought of as a way to hide in plain sight. A skilled camouflage user will be able to change their entire persona, including body language, when necessary.

Subliminal Instructions

When it comes to manipulation, we must remember that there are two types: positive manipulation and negative manipulation. These will use the same techniques along the way, but the intention behind them will be slightly different, and this is how we get each type.

We spent some time investigating negative manipulation and how it treats and harms the target. As long as the manipulator can get what they want and use the target as a tool, they will do so—and it makes no difference to them whether the target is harmed in the process or not. The manipulator will be content as long as they see themselves as the victor or in command.

There is now a type of manipulation that is regarded as more positive. It employs the same techniques that we see in negative manipulation, but it will do so with better intentions. This type of manipulator still works to get what they want from the target, but they have a conscience and do not want to harm the other person. This type of manipulation is often beneficial to both parties or is more beneficial to the target than the manipulator.

Persuasion

Before delving into the skillset known as persuasion, keep in mind that there are two types of persuasion. On the one hand, there is regular everyday persuasiveness. When people discuss persuasive writing techniques, they are referring to this type of persuasion. It can also withstand ethical or morally motivated social pressure. Dark persuasion, on the other hand, is more in line with the topic of this book.

This is the type of persuasion that is motivated by personal gain rather than ethics or morality, the type of persuasion that has no qualms about negatively impacting people's lives. It is the persuasion of conmen, corrupt politicians, and unethical lawyers. All groups of people who, you guessed it, engage in dark psychology regularly.

CHAPTER 5
THE 10 BEST TECHNIQUES OF DARK PSYCHOLOGY

Love Bombing

When beginning their interactions with their victims, many emotional manipulators will use love bombing as a technique. It will entail an intense, sudden, and forceful display of a large number of positive emotions to a victim. When discussing CEM, this may appear to be counterintuitive at first. Why would the manipulator work increase positivity in the beginning if they are trying to cause harm to someone? It's because doing so can help them achieve their own goals.

The idea behind using love bombing is to elicit an intense feeling of affection, trust, and compliance from the victim toward their manipulator. The extent to which love bombing will be used, as well as the person on whom it will be used, will frequently be determined by how the manipulator assesses the situation. A victim who appears lonely, in need of support, comfort, and despondent is more likely to be love-bombed and with greater intensity than others. If the victim is more grounded, they will require a less intense, and possibly more subtle, method of love bombing.

Passive-Aggressive Retaliation

Passive-aggressive revenge is similar to cold treatment in that the manipulator ignores the victim partially as a form of punishment. The only difference is that instead of completely cutting off communication, the manipulators act obstinately. They put on fake smiles to appear unoffended, but their actions, such as body language, tell a different story. If the oppressed person approaches the manipulator, the manipulator fabricates a reason to move away.

Similarly, if the victim attempts to communicate with them, the manipulator may respond angrily. They will pretend to forget things to punish the other person. Worse, rather than discussing issues with the affected individual, they resort to backstabbing.

Reality Is Perplexing

When people are in the hands of skilled manipulators, their differing opinions are transformed into irrationality. Simply put, if you disagree with a toxic person, they will reframe whatever you said to make it appear heinous and absurd. For example, if you confront them about speaking rudely to you, they will say things like, "So you think you're perfect, unlike me, huh?"

This is referred to as confusing or misrepresenting reality. Its goal is to instil guilt, even though all a person did was express their feelings.

A manipulator believes they can read people's minds and determine their intentions. This explains why they make decisions based on their reality rather than facts. This is referred to as putting words in people's mouths and blaming them for it. Manipulators, according to psychology, understand their dark nature and will move quickly to accuse others of painting them as dark-natured. In short, the act of perverting reality is a form of self-defence for them.

Denial of Reality

The fear of losing one's sanity is one of the most terrifying experiences a person can have. This is bad enough if it is explained by something the victim understands, such as a side effect of stress in their lives. However, if the insanity feeling is induced by the emotional manipulator, this can be extremely unsettling.

Reality denial refers to a set of techniques used in CEM to destroy the victim's sanity to achieve selfish goals. How this occurs and its impact will vary depending on the method that works best for the manipulator.

One of the central concepts of reality denial is that it occurs gradually. If the manipulator tries to do everything at once, the victim will notice and will flee. As a result, the manipulator is unlikely to immediately aim to destroy their victim's sanity. You will almost certainly be detected if you achieve this type of result.

Projection

Projection is the act of refusing to see one's flaws and using any available tactic to blame others for them. This mechanism shifts a person's negative behaviour and attributes it to someone else. While everyone engages in projection on occasion, a manipulator uses it excessively, which adds up to psychological abuse. Instead of accepting their wrongdoings, imperfections, and flaws, a manipulator dumps them on others cruelly and painfully. As a result, the manipulator will not stop the behaviour to seek correction or improvement, and their victims will feel ashamed and responsible for something they did not do.

Insults delivered inadvertently

Insults and name-calling are direct manifestations of abuse and aggression. A toxic person is aware of this and will use mind tricks to avoid being blamed for insulting or calling their subject names. As a result, they will consider the raw insult and devise a way to disguise it with other words, making it appear less brutal. To confuse the subject, insults may be delivered covertly, such as with sarcasm and a calm voice tone. The subject may believe they are receiving advice, solutions, assistance, or instruction when, in fact, they are being insulted. The manipulator, on the other hand, is aware that their intentions are not genuine and are intended to undermine the victim's abilities and confidence. Backhanded compliments are another term for covert insults. Regardless of how sugar-coated the insults are, the victims are aware that they have been undermined. This causes pain and hurt, especially when the manipulator is someone close to you, such as a lover, sibling, friend, boss, teacher, or colleague.

Triangulation

Triangulation is yet another powerful tool for manipulating people. A third party is involved in the manipulator's relationship with another person. They want their subject to be aware that a third party can be used to replace them at any time. Once insecure, the victim is compelled to comply with all of the manipulator's wishes for fear of losing them and/or being replaced.

Although the third party is not directly depicted as equal to the victim, the manipulator ensures that the victim is aware that someone else exists whom the toxic person adores. If the victim inquires about the third party, they are labelled as insecure, jealous, or insensitive. If it reaches this point, the manipulator has gained control of the subject. The subject, on the other hand, makes an effort to please the manipulator to keep them around.

Treatment in Complete Silence

Withholding or stonewalling are other terms for silent treatment. It is the act in which a person cuts communication and then uses physical or emotional withdrawal to express their disappointment after feeling wronged. This is something we mostly witnessed as children. When we were kids, if we were denied something or punished by our parents, we would sulk and withdraw from them until they made it up to us. I'm sure you remember this. We were once little manipulators!

We could have been manipulators, but it wasn't toxic. When cold treatment begins to convey contempt and belittlement, it becomes toxic manipulation. A manipulator sends the message that a person is not worthy of their time, love, or attention.

The implication is that the victim is unimportant and that they can exist without them. If they are successful, the victim feels humiliated and powerless. Cold treatment is referred to as torture by psychologists because humans require recognition of their existence, particularly from those closest to them. While cold treatment may appear to be a lack of communication, it is strong communication that you must either play the manipulator's game or continue to suffer.

Blackmailing

Another popular technique used in the manipulation process is blackmail. This is the use of unjustified threats to gain an advantage or have one's demands met. It is also a form of coercion. The manipulator employs this technique to force a subject to do what they want or to obtain something they desire. For this method to work, the manipulator must first study the victim. They discover personal characteristics and secrets that could endanger the subject. A man, for example, might threaten to reveal a dirty secret about a lady if they do not have sex with them. Some manipulators may go so far as to threaten subjects or their loved ones with physical harm if they do not comply with their demands.

Humiliation

Shaming is a powerful tool used by manipulators to undermine victims' self-esteem and willpower. A manipulator researches and targets the subjects that the victim is proud of. By belittling and/or making the victim feel as if they made bad decisions and should be ashamed of them, the victim's pride and sense of self are diminished. Toxic people are interested in people's scars and wounds because they can be used as a powerful arsenal when the time comes. Manipulators can be so ruthless that they will target wounds like childhood abuse to traumatize their victims.

CHAPTER 6
6 ADVANCED MENTAL MANIPULATION TECHNIQUES

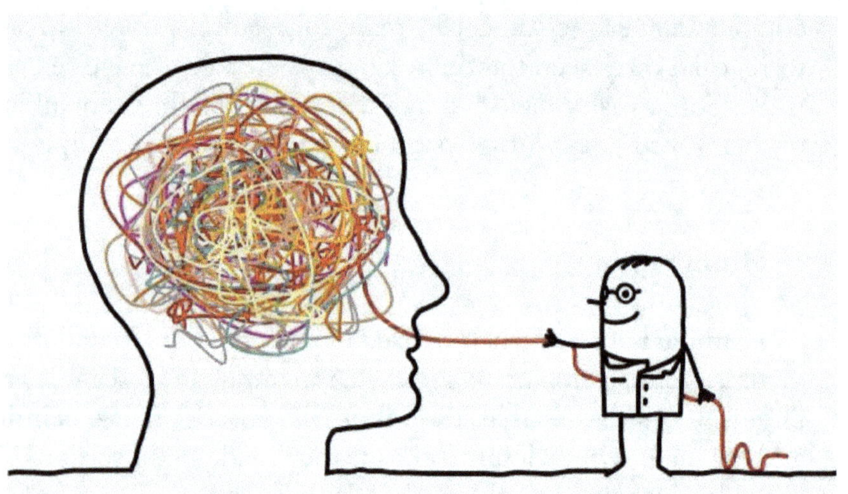

Gaslighting

This is a deceptive technique used to erode and distort a person's sense of reality. It erodes a person's ability to trust themselves. In practice, the manipulator gains the upper hand by convincing their victims that they are imagining things that did not occur.

They will deny that anything happened and attempt to make the victim believe they are insane. When gaslighting is used, the subject must decide whether to trust the manipulator or stick to what they believe happened. At this point, the manipulator enters the scene with reasons to persuade them that the victims are delusory. Many times, the victim is so deeply affected that they begin to doubt their sanity.

Gaslighting is a tactic of gradual manipulation that grows in severity and frequency over time. As the severity increases, the victim suffers from confusion, depression, and anxiety. When they finally begin to question their sanity and reality, their self-esteem plummets, and they become reliant on the manipulator. At this point, the manipulators have gotten their way and can exercise dominance or reap whatever benefits they desired.

When a person becomes angry and says hurtful things during an argument, this is an example of gaslighting. After the argument has subsided, the angry person denies ever being angry and accuses the other party of lying.

Cancelling Willpower

Willpower is defined as the determination, drive, control, discipline, or self-effort required to complete a task. According to research, people who have a high level of willpower are better at controlling their attention, emotions, and behaviours. It is their distinct ability to manage their lives that allows them to excel at goal achievement. Willpower, like self-esteem, is threatening to the manipulator because it affects their rate of success in controlling their potential victims. As a result, they use tactics to cancel a person's willpower before invading their minds, just as they do to attack self-esteem.

Reading in the Cold

Cold reading is widely regarded as a con artist's best friend.

It creates the illusion of mind reading and magical abilities without utilizing actual supernatural power. It is frequently used by those who make a living from fortune-telling and psychic acts. Many people have been completely sold on the act, which is typically performed by someone who excels at reading others, has acquired enough general knowledge, and has practised enough to deliver a very convincing performance.

The Benefits of a Home Court

When someone is attempting to manipulate a new target, they will use any method at their disposal to gain the upper hand in the situation.

The manipulator may decide to invite the target to a meeting or find another method of interaction in a physical space where the manipulator has complete dominance and control. This is why the manipulator may decide to hold the meeting at their home, office, or somewhere else the manipulator is familiar with but the target is unaware of.

The victim, on the other hand, is completely out of their element. They are pleased that the manipulator wishes to meet with them and may consider it very friendly that the manipulator is willing to choose the location, viewing this as a very hospitable thing to do. But, in reality, it's all for the manipulator's benefit, just like everything else they do. It enables them to gain an advantage over the target from the start.

Nitpicking

Nitpicking is also known as moving the goalposts or looking for flaws where none exist. Nitpicking is a type of criticism that, rather than helping a person, degrades them in dark psychology. A manipulator will shift the goalposts whenever their subject mentions an accomplishment that they are proud of. They intend to make their subjects feel worthless, underachieved, and failed. When the subject opens up about something they believe is good for them during this process, the manipulator raises more expectations to discredit their subjects. They recognize this by raising the bar above what their victims have come to expect. They can make them feel dissatisfied and worthless.

Threats

One of the most damaging things a manipulator can go through is having their false sense of entitlement, grandiosity, and superiority challenged in any way. When a victim is suspected of committing such a violation, they are threatened. The manipulator resorts to making unreasonable demands on the victim while threatening punishment for failing to meet their standards. If the victim believes the threat will have a significant impact on them, they have no choice but to comply with the manipulator's wishes.

When a manipulator disagrees with someone, they try to take away the subject's right to make decisions. To accomplish this, they employ a strategy that instils fear in the other person if they disagree or fail to meet their demands.

When they disagree with someone, they issue selfish ultimatums along the lines of "if you don't do this, then I will do this!"

CHAPTER 7
MANIPULATION IN THE EMOTIONAL AND AFFECTIVE SPHERE AND POWERFUL HIDDEN EMOTIONAL MANIPULATION TECHNIQUES

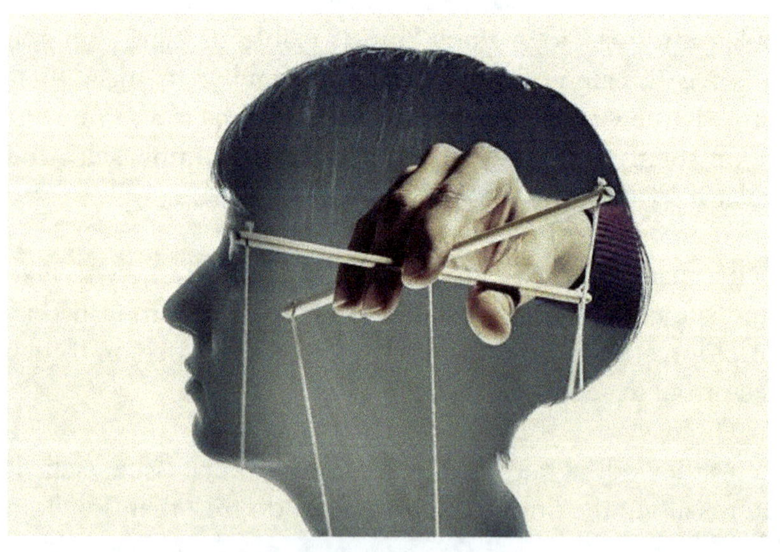

Manipulative Relationship Characteristics

According to one theory, emotional manipulation is essentially a one-sided activity in which the manipulator expends all of the effort to create, execute, and sustain a manipulative relationship.

These kinds of relationships typically have three distinguishing characteristics:

    a. Concealment: The manipulator's true motivations—aggression and control—are hidden behind friendly and helpful behaviour.

    b. Profiling: The manipulator will have studied the victim's vulnerabilities to exploit them more effectively. This type of predatory behaviour has gotten much worse in today's world of surveillance and social networking sites.

    c. Amorality: The manipulator will have a high level of amorality and a lack of remorse, both of which enable ruthless, cunning, and treacherous behaviour.

We frequently believe that a simple, polite request to stop harmful, rude, or disruptive behaviour will suffice to end predatory or violative behaviour.

Even if we are correct, dark triad personalities who lack empathy find it easy to engage in immoral behaviour.

Worse, rather than feeling remorse for their actions, they frequently feel a great sense of joy, victory, and accomplishment. Such reactions, as the saying goes, add insult to injury.

Furthermore, in today's competitive business environment, dishonest and illegal behaviour may be rewarded. Meanwhile, the efforts of hardworking, honest employees may go unnoticed, and their complaints of abuse may result in punishments meted out to them rather than the perpetrators.

How Are Emotional Manipulation Tactics Used in Dark Psychology Nowadays?

Nobody wants to be the victim of manipulation, but it happens all the time. We may not be directly exposed to someone in the Dark Psychology. Even so, we face dark psychology tactics daily with ordinary people like you and me. Such strategies are frequently used in advertisements, web ads, sales techniques, and even our boss's actions. If you have children (especially teenagers), you will almost certainly encounter these strategies as your children experiment with behaviours to get what they want and try to gain autonomy for themselves.

Covert manipulation and dark persuasion are frequently used by people you trust and love. Here are some of the most common techniques used by ordinary people:

- Best wishes, companionship, or buttering someone up to make a request are all ways to show love.

- Untruths, distortions, partial truths, and false tales are all examples of falsification.

- Love denial is the act of withholding one's attention and affection.

- Withdrawal symptoms include avoiding people or using a silent treatment.

- Choice restraint: Providing options that separate you from the option that no one wants to take.

- Reverse psychology is when you say or do something to inspire someone to do the opposite of what you want.

- Semantic manipulation is when you use terms that are meant to have a shared or collective meaning, but the manipulator later tells you that they have a different definition and interpretation of the conversation. Words have a lot of power and influence. You will be able to avoid being manipulated if you are aware of these. These are meant to remind us all how simple it is to use those strategies to get what we want.

- They keep their home-court advantage: Being on your home turf, whether it's your actual home or just a favourite coffee shop, can be inspiring. If the other people frequently insist on meeting within their domain, they may try to create a power imbalance. They claim ownership of that space, putting you at a disadvantage.

- They get very close very quickly: Emotional manipulators may skip a few steps in the typical get-to-know-you process. They "share" their deepest flaws and secrets. Nonetheless, they are attempting to make you feel different for you to share your secrets. They may later use your sensitivities against you. As an example: "I get the impression that we only communicate on an intense level. That has never occurred before." " "I've never had someone share their dream with me like you. We are truly meant to be in this together.

- They allow you to reveal your secrets first: This is a common tactic in some business relationships, but it can also occur in personal ones. If you want to establish control, you should ask questions about sampling early on so you can share your thoughts and concerns. With their secret plan in mind, they can then use your answers to influence your choices.

- They distort the facts: Emotional manipulators are experts at distorting reality to confuse you with lies, fibs, or misstatements. They can exaggerate incidents to appear more vulnerable. They may also overestimate their role in a dispute to gain your support. As an example: "I asked her a question about the project, and she came up to me, yelling about how I'd never done anything to help her, but you know I do, right? "I cried all night and didn't get much sleep."

- The subject you to intellectual bullying: When you ask a question, you may be bombarded with numbers, jargon, or evidence, and you may be subjected to emotional manipulation.

- Some of them believe they are the experts, and they impose their "knowledge" on you. This is especially common in financial or sales situations.

- If you ask a question, they make you feel bad: An emotional manipulator may respond aggressively or try to draw you into an argument if you ask questions or offer advice. This method allows them to manipulate your options and influence your decisions. They can also use the situation to make you feel guilty for raising your concerns in the first place.

- "I don't understand why you don't trust me," for example.

- "You already know I'm an emotional person. I can't help but wonder where you are all the time.

- They always prefer to talk about their problems: If you're having a bad day, an emotional manipulator may take advantage of the situation and ask you questions. The goal is to disprove what you're feeling. It is, so you are compelled to focus on manipulators and focus your emotional energy on their problems.

- They are always criticizing you: Emotional manipulators may reject or weaken you if you lack the concept of wit or sarcasm.

- Their remarks are intended to erode your self-esteem.

- They're supposed to make fun of you and push you to the sidelines. The manipulator also revealed their flaws. As an example: " "Do you think that suit is a little provocative for a client meeting? That's one way to get the wallet, I suppose." "Everything you do is based on what you eat."

Emotional Manipulation Techniques with Hidden Power

Psychologists have identified a wide range of more subtle variations within these major categories of emotional manipulation techniques that we all likely encounter daily. Among these methods are:

Lying: Because Dark Triad personalities, particularly psychopaths, are skilled at lying and cheating, we may not detect their intent until it is too late. Be wary of those who have a history of dishonesty.

Lying by omission: This is a subtler form of lying.
The predator may not say anything false, but he or she may withhold information that is required to cause you to fail.

Denial: Emotional manipulation often causes damage after the fact. When confronted with evidence of dishonesty and abuse, a person's refusal to admit wrongdoing can cause even more psychological harm.

Rationalization: The rise of popular news media has resulted in the growth of public relations and marketing firms that create "spin" to deflect criticism in both political and corporate settings. Rationalization is a type of spin in which a manipulator rationalizes their abuse.

Minimization: Minimization, like rationalization, is a type of denial in which the predator downplays the gravity of their offence.

Selective attention and/or inattention: Manipulators will pick and choose which parts of an argument or debate to consider to represent only their points of view.

Manipulators frequently resist giving direct answers to questions, especially when confronted by their victims.

Instead, they will change the subject or divert the conversation to another topic.

Evasion: A manipulative person confronted with their guilt will frequently completely evade responsibility by using long rambling responses filled with so-called "weasel words," such as "most people would say," "according to my sources," or other phrases that falsely legitimize their excuses.

To discourage further inquiries or resolution, many manipulative people will make implied threats.

Guilt-tripping: A true form of emotional manipulation in which the manipulator exploits the victim's integrity and conscientiousness by accusing them of being too selfish, irresponsible, or not caring enough.

Shaming: While shaming can be used to effect social change when large corporations or governments implement abusive or discriminatory policies, manipulators may try to intimidate their victims by using harsh criticism, sarcastic comments, or insults to make them feel bad.

Blaming the victim: This tactic is becoming more popular. When a victim accuses a predator of abuse, the predator will try to turn the situation around by fabricating a scenario in which the victim is solely responsible for the harm that has been done to them. By complaining about the violation, the predator may also try to accuse the victim of being the aggressor.

Playing the victim: Using the opposite tactic of blaming the victim, the predator will entice a conscientious person into a trap by pretending to be grievously injured and cultivating feelings of sympathy. The real plan, however, is to exploit the conscientious person's caring nature by playing on their emotions.

Playing the servant is a common tactic in environments with a strict, well-established chain of command, such as the military. Predators become adept at manipulating this system by assuming the personas of suffering and nobility, in which their bad actions are justified as duty, obedience, and honour.

Seduction is a technique that does not always involve sexual conquest or intimacy. Emotional predators may use flattery and charm to persuade others to do their bidding, and they frequently target people with low self-esteem.

In psychotherapy, this term is referred to as projection.

Predators who employ this tactic will seek victims to use as scapegoats.

When the manipulator commits an error and is confronted, they will "project" their guilt onto the victim in an attempt to make the victim appear to be the guilty party.

Feigning innocence: This technique can be used as part of a denial strategy. When confronted, the manipulator will "play innocent," claiming that any violation was unintentional or that they were not the party who committed the violation. A skilled manipulator who lacks morality and empathy can be very effective at sowing doubt.

Confusion feigning: This technique can also be used as part of a denial strategy. When confronted with questions, the manipulator will "play dumb" or pretend to be perplexed about the central point of the conflict or dispute. The manipulator hopes to undermine their victim's confidence by creating confusion.

Peer pressure: The manipulator will put pressure on their victim to change their behaviour or attitude by making claims, whether true or false, that the victim's friends, associates, or "everyone else" is doing something.

CHAPTER 8
HOW TO TELL IF YOU ARE EMOTIONALLY MANIPULATED AND TIPS FOR OVERCOMING AND ESCAPING FROM TOXIC PEOPLE OR RELATIONSHIPS

Toxicity, like mould, spreads over time. It can spread to you if you are not careful. Consider this: if you've ever had a small pint of raspberries that mostly looked good but one of them was a little fuzzy, you understand the need to remove the toxic part. You are well aware that if you do not remove it as soon as possible, you will face a major problem: the mould will spread to the healthy, perfect raspberries. This is a major issue—if you want to enjoy your raspberries without them going bad, you must remove the mouldy ones to protect the fresh ones. Toxic relationships in your life are no different—they are mouldy and will only cause you problems.

1. What Exactly Is a Toxic Relationship?

Toxic relationships are problematic ones. It is critical to remember that they are distinguished by the presence of destructive or toxic behaviours within them. You have toxic relationships in your life that cause you pain. They make you feel ill, both physically and psychologically. When you are in a toxic relationship, you lack everything that makes a relationship strong—trust. You are unreliable. You're heartless. This is a major issue for both of you.

The toxic person is most likely unaware that they are toxic. They are usually already dysfunctional as a result of a poor upbringing. They are sometimes aware of their tendencies but do not care. Other times, with intensive therapy and a strong desire to change, they may be able to figure it out over time. Whatever the case, the toxic relationship should be terminated, at least for the time it will take for the individual to work on themselves.

Toxic relationships are the source of the majority of people's problems. It can be difficult to determine who is toxic and bringing you down.

2. Managing Toxic People

Dealing with toxic people in your life entails five steps, each of which is detailed below: Recognize Toxic Individuals.

The first step toward resolving a problem is recognizing that you have one. They could be hovering over your life like a bird of prey about to dive for its prey. Or you could already be imprisoned in their talons and be unaware of it. Whatever your situation is, the first step is to identify such individuals. Increase Your Self-Esteem.

Others must see you as a human being, just like them. They must perceive you to be valuable, dignified, and honourable. They must see you as deserving of praise from others. But, if you don't value your self-worth and self-esteem, how can you expect others to?

3. Communication that works

You should be able to recognize toxic people by now. You were able to identify specific toxicity traits in them. You've realized Chloe has a lot of negative feelings for you. Charlie's lies, you know, will put the devils to shame. You can be certain that

John's desire to dominate was the catalyst for his threats and attack on you a few weeks ago. You have grasped all of these concepts. What comes next?

4. Use a Mediator

Wherever possible, a third party can be involved. But you're not bringing them to judge; instead, they're here to mediate between you two. They are not pointing fingers, but rather facilitating effective communication between you two.

5. Accept Responsibility

You may have provoked another person's behaviour toward you. You've read about toxic people's characteristics. What makes you think you don't have those qualities? What makes you believe you're perfect? Some people may not know how to effectively communicate their reservations to you, so they simply choose to let them show in their interactions with you.

Getting Rid of a Toxic Relationship

The "when" comes before the "how," which is a logical order. If you believe that every time you identify someone toxic in your life, you must eliminate them, you are mistaken. Yes, I am referring to the fact that you are still learning how to deal with toxic people. As is customary, I will be succinct, precise, and practical.

When to Call It a Day

To begin, you must be able to recognize when a relationship is ready to end. This occurs when it has irreparably broken down, i.e., when all attempts to salvage it have failed for any number of reasons. Someone promising to be better but only getting worse after you give them a second chance is one example.

How to Get Out of a Toxic Relationship

To comprehend how you will learn what to do in two significant situations.

The two scenarios are dependent on how close you are to the other person.

For Near Relatives

Your parents, siblings, in-laws, cousins, spouse, and other close relatives are examples of close relatives. In this case, you keep the bond that binds you while keeping your distance from the person. Assume it's your parents who you've finally realized are toxic to you.

The parental bond is extremely important and should never be completely severed. This is in appreciation of everything our parents have done for us.

You keep your distance by not allowing them to influence or interfere in your affairs. You can always drop by regularly to check on them, their health, and how they are doing—this is how you maintain your bond with them. However, never allow them to influence your decisions. Stop them if they try, and politely excuse yourself if they don't.

In the case of your spouse, especially if children are involved, you must exercise caution and proceed slowly. There's a reason it's a "for-better-or-worse" situation. You must persevere for a little longer for one simple reason: when two elephants fight, the grasses are trampled. Think carefully about the impact of a divorce on your children and their upbringing, and don't make any hasty decisions. This is why I first recommend marriage counselling.

When you bring up the idea of therapy with your partner, make it clear that you are doing so because you care about your marriage and your children. If possible, offer to cover the financial costs—this demonstrates sincerity. If therapy fails, you may want to think about other options, such as a shared mentor or another mediator. If all attempts to repair the situation fail, staying in such a toxic relationship can harm the children. It's possible that you'd be better off raising them while you're apart. Others have succeeded in this area, and you can as well.

Regarding Non-Relatives

This category includes your boss, coworkers, fiancé(e), girlfriend or boyfriend, and so on. In the case of your fiancé(e), you know it's time to call it quits. It's pointless to be together if your relationship is rife with toxicity. In the case of your friends, such relationships must be terminated. In both cases, inform them of your decision and the reasons for your decision.

Communicate it. "Chloe, you remember our conversation at Point Café last month, don't you?" You said you'd change, but I don't believe you have. I can think of two instances where you did exactly what you said you would stop doing. I've made it clear that I won't have a friend who thinks poorly of me. We appear to be better off on our own and with others. This is not intended to be an argument. I'm just informing you of my decision. May the odds be on our side. Thank you for a fantastic time so far."

In the case of a coworker or member of your team, you should also inform them that you two will continue to interact professionally, but anything beyond that will no longer occur.

CHAPTER 9
MANIPULATION AND CONVERSATIONAL HYPNOSIS

What Exactly Is Hypnosis?

Hypnosis is a psychological technique that involves inducing a state of consciousness in which the individual loses the ability to act of their own volition. When a person is in a hypnotic state, they lose touch with reality and only focus or operate in a different world. Through visualization, hypnosis creates a new world/environment in the individual's mind. In the other world, a person can be heard conversing with other people. When a person is hypnotized, they are extremely receptive to suggestions or directions.

Hypnosis is used in therapy to help people recover from a variety of ailments.

Although hypnosis has been practised for a long time, it remains one of the most contentious therapeutic techniques.

While some psychologists believe that a person in a hypnotic state has no control over their actions, others believe that a person's free will cannot be completely lost.

In general, hypnosis can occur naturally or be induced. Natural hypnosis occurs without the person's knowledge or request.

According to psychologists, an adult human being must experience a hypnotic state at least once per day. Later, we'll look at some examples of hypnotic states. That being said, a naturally occurring hypnotic state cannot be used to control your mind and actions. When it comes to mind control, the induced hypnotic state works well.

Music is one method of inducing a hypnotic state in a person. If you play music with a tempo or rhythm of 45–72 beats per minute, you will most likely transport a person's mind into a hypnotic state. The message contained within such music has the potential to transform a person's thinking processes and ideas. This is because the music has the same beat as your heartbeat. As a result, every beat of the song is perfectly timed with your thoughts.

Guided hypnosis is another option for induced hypnosis.

The most common type of hypnosis is guided hypnosis, which takes place at a therapist's table. A hypnotist is the only person who can perform hypnosis. Hypnotists guide the subject through a visual journey that can be used to change the subject's way of thinking.

To achieve a heightened state of awareness, also known as trance, hypnosis employs guided relaxation and intense concentration. In this state of mind, the person's attention is so focused that they may not notice or recognize anything that is going on around them. You've probably seen someone crossing the street with their eyes glued to their phone, almost getting hit by a car. This is a person in a natural hypnotic state. You do not feel or experience the world around you when you are in a hypnotic state. Everything is centred on the new world you've created in your mind. You must allow yourself to return to the real world to resume a normal life. Hypnosis is distinguished by two factors:

Suggestion therapy: Suggestion therapy forces a person to respond to suggestions. When a hypnotist performs hypnosis on a person, that person only focuses on the hypnotist's suggestions. Hypnosis has been used to help people change their habits, such as quitting smoking and biting their nails.

Analysis: A skilled hypnotist can use hypnosis to achieve results that are out of the ordinary. For example, the hypnotist can lead the individual through a relaxed state of events to extract vital information. The analysis procedure assists the therapist in determining the underlying cause of mental or social disorders.

How Does Hypnosis Work?

Hypnosis works because the person being hypnotized ultimately wants to be suggested to. It is a state in which the hypnotist carefully guides them through their mind, gradually but steadily assisting them in determining what they want. When you understand this, you begin to see hypnosis for what it is: a way for two people to collaborate to achieve a goal. When you learn how to do this effectively, you can usually persuade the other person to do amazing things. For example, hypnosis is frequently used to assist people in accomplishing tasks that they did not believe they were capable of in the first place. One common example is assisting people in losing weight when they want to.

To be able to lose weight, you must first be able to persuade your mind to do so. Some people struggle with this and, as a result, they never lose weight. You can, however, make it happen with hypnosis.

Hypnosis works because it allows you to postpone your unconscious thought processes. Remember how we talked about how NLP worked exactly that way?

You can encourage your mind to change your unconscious thoughts by telling yourself that you need to change them and then doing so.

Consider the following scenario: you want to lose weight. Your subconscious mind, on the other hand, believes you will fail. Perhaps you've failed in the past, or you believe you're too weak-willed or otherwise incapable of making it happen. Whatever the reason, you are convinced that you are the problem and that you will not lose weight. So, what do you think will happen next? Naturally, if you don't believe you can lose weight, you won't be able to. You set yourself up for failure by defeating yourself. As a result, you're stuck—you can't change what you were doing, and you can't figure out how to avoid that problem in the future.

However, hypnosis allows you to enter the subconscious and unconscious mind and change those thoughts. Instead of telling yourself that you will never be able to lose weight, remind yourself that you can lose weight—you just have to be diligent enough to make it happen. You can solve that problem, and in doing so, you can convince yourself that you can do better—than you can lose that weight.

You know that now that your subconscious mind has been redirected in a new direction, you will be able to better trust yourself and your thoughts.

You will be able to ensure that you take the time to lose weight at that time because your mind will believe that you can.

As you can see, hypnosis and NLP are similar in that you use a partnership between two people to alter thought processes to change behaviours. When you do this, you know you have the ability to change your behaviours with ease.

NLP and hypnosis are both powerful methods of influencing the mind that can be used in different ways to achieve the same end goal.

How to Handle Hypnosis

While being in a hypnotic state is beneficial to performers and athletes, it is also extremely hazardous. You are 25% more suggestible than usual when you are under guided hypnosis or music-induced hypnosis. In other words, you are easily swayed by other people's suggestions and may act against your will. As a result, you must exercise caution when allowing anyone to perform hypnosis on you. Unless it is a trusted professional therapist, you should never allow anyone to lead you into hypnosis. If you notice that someone is attempting to induce a hypnotic state in your mind, stop communicating with them and avoid them completely. Allowing people to make such moves around you makes it very easy to become trapped in the world of hypnosis against your will.

How to Utilize Hypnosis

Keeping this in mind, there are several techniques you can use to covertly hypnotize someone while conversing with them. These techniques will assist you in inducing a hypnotic trance in someone. Once in this trance, you can issue "commands" to your subject, which they will obey if they are suggestible.

A pattern interrupt is the first hypnosis technique. Humans are similar to computers. When a computer encounters faulty coding or an unexpected command, it may become stuck in a "loop."

The human mind works similarly. Our brains enjoy running through familiar patterns or rituals, and when they come across something unexpected in the middle of either, they become confused. During this state of confusion, the individual is vulnerable to any commands that may be issued. Here's an example of how to do a pattern interrupt: When someone extends their hand to shake yours, take a step forward and place your palm flat on their chest instead of taking their hand. This will confuse the person, giving you a few seconds to issue commands to them.

The second covert hypnosis technique feels nothing like hypnosis at all. It's not very theatrical, but it's incredibly effective. This is known as the "imagine method," and it simply entails using the word "imagine." For example, if you were trying to persuade a romantic partner to accept a job offer, you could say, "Imagine how much better our lives would be if you took the job." You are engaging the visual part of the person's brain by asking them to imagine this possibility, making it far easier for you to influence them. When you use the image method, your communicative partner may believe they have made up their mind when you have made it up for them.

The Zeigarnik Effect is the next hypnotic technique. This technique is similar to a pattern interrupt in that both only work if they temporarily confuse your communicative partner. The premise of the Zeigarnik Effect is that the human brain craves completion. If something is left unfinished, the mind becomes "stuck" while attempting to mentally complete whatever has been left undone. While the subject's mind is "stuck" in this state, the hypnotist can give them commands or insert suggestions into their subconscious mind. If you want to use this effect, start by telling a very detailed, intriguing story to a friend.

Stop for a few seconds about halfway through the story. The silence that follows is the time when you must implant suggestions or commands into your subject's mind. Once again, it is the confusion that causes the subject to enter a trance-like state.

You can even induce a full-fledged, unconscious trance in a communicative partner without ever touching them. This appears to be stage hypnosis, which you may have seen before. Approach the person you want to hypnotize and strike up a conversation with them. Maintain a lively discussion for a few moments before beginning to yawn and telling your communicative partner how tired you are. From now on, you must keep an eye on their actions. Continue to mention how tired you are, and watch as they become drowsier and drowsier. You can sneak in the "sleep" command once they are completely drowsy. This can be accomplished by saying something like,

"Keep feeling like that once you're asleep." Your communicative partner should become unconscious without too much repetition (make sure you catch them). They should be highly suggestible in this state. You will be able to wake them up simply by commanding them to do so.

Of course, other people aren't the only ones who can hypnotize. You, too, can hypnotize yourself. If you're trying to quit smoking or lose weight, self-hypnosis can be extremely beneficial.

To hypnotize yourself, simply sit or lie down somewhere comfortable and close your eyes. Close your eyes and begin focusing on your head until you are fully aware of its dimensions and weight. After you've finished with your head, move on to your neck and shoulders, working your way down until you reach your toes. You have entered a hypnotic state when you are fully aware of your body. You can give yourself commands (for example, "I will stop smoking") while in this hypnotic state, and you should find it easier to comply with these commands once you have returned to your normal state of consciousness.

CHAPTER 10
WAYS TO PROTECT YOURSELF FROM MIND CONTROL

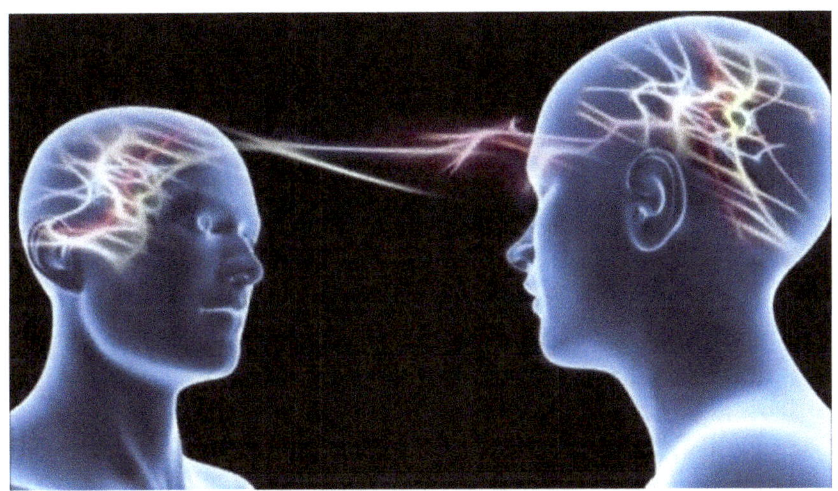

Mind control refers to a variety of psychological phenomena, including mind control, coercive control, brainwashing, coercive persuasion, malignant use of group dynamics, and many others.

It's a psychological theory with a lot of different names. The many names given to the theory are a clear indication of a lack of agreement, which allows for distortion and confusion, especially in the hands of those who intend to use it covertly for their selfish interests.

However, one can agree that mind control easily falls under the umbrella of influence and persuasion, which deals with how people change the beliefs and behaviours of others. While some may argue that manipulation encompasses everything, it is important to note the gaps in this argument.

Mind control creates a new pseudo-identity or pseudo-personality for the person, which can be used to benefit others or the person himself in a variety of ways. Mind control, for example, can be used to help addicts while also being used in bad and/or unethical ways.

Understanding how these work can help you use them when you need to influence the other person or be aware of the manipulation that may be used against you. Some of the most common mind control techniques that can be used are as follows:

Isolation

Isolation is the first technique that can be used in mind control. Humans are extremely social beings. They enjoy talking with others, going out in public, spending time with close friends and family, and engaging in more social activities.
When we take away this social aspect from many people, it can change their perspective on life.

Criticism

Criticism is frequently used as a tool for isolation, but it can also be used on its own. Manipulators enjoy using criticism because it makes the target feel insecure and as if they are doing something wrong. The criticism can range from the clothes a person wears to how they look, who their friends are, and even their beliefs.

Peer Influence and Social Proof

We all want to feel like we belong to a group. Some people are obsessed with fitting in, and they will go to great lengths to be the life of the party, to be liked, and so much more—and even those who are more introverted, who prefer to spend more time at home rather than going out and partying and socializing all of the time, want to make sure that others like them and that they fit in.

Fear of Being Isolated

Nobody wants to be isolated. They want to feel like they are a part of something bigger. They want to feel accepted and as if they are a part of something. This is never more evident than when we encounter a newcomer. When someone is new to town, school, work, or anywhere else, you will notice that they are trying to figure out how to fit in and get the group to accept them.

Repetition

The more we hear about something, the more likely it is to stick with us. A manipulator can use this method of mind control to their advantage if they keep repeating their message and using the same tools on their intended target to get what they want.

Fatigue

How good are your decision-making skills when you're tired? Do you find that you just want to go to bed, which causes you to be tired, irritable, and moody? Often, your decisions will be questionable, and you may agree to things that you would never agree to if you had gotten enough sleep.

Creating a New Identity

This is more likely to happen during more extreme forms of manipulation, but it is still something we need to look into.

In some cases, the manipulator alters their target's identity. This ensures that they get more of what they want from the person. If they can persuade the target to abandon their old way of thinking and doing things, leaving them with a blank slate, they can go through and fill in that blank slate with whatever they want.

CHAPTER 11
10 STRATEGIES FOR MASS MANIPULATION BY THE MEDIA

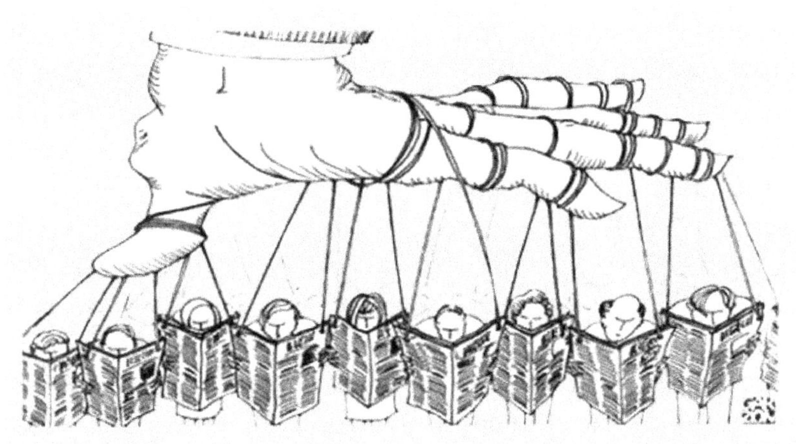

Distraction

The distraction strategy is intended to divert the target population's attention away from important issues in their lives. To keep people distracted, media outlets can flood the news with stories about insignificant issues. The main goal is to keep people's minds occupied and keep them distracted. As a result, people will stop questioning why the media isn't looking into specific issues. People will even forget about the real issues as a result of this process.

Problem-Reaction-Solution

This method is similar to how politicians try to entice voters during election season. Normally, the population is tested first. The first step will be to spread rumours, after which an evaluation will be conducted to see how the general public reacts. Following the creation of a problem, the second phase entails offering a solution to the problem. The manipulators will be regarded as heroes by the general public.

Gradualism

This is the process of manipulating people into accepting some socially unjust decisions. The population is gradually manipulated. The gradual manipulation could take many years.

Differing

Another strategy used by the media is different; in this case, people present some unpopular decisions and may emphasize that the decisions should be implemented because the general population will benefit significantly. The public may genuinely believe everything, and they may make some sacrifices in the hope of bringing about significant changes. Politicians, for example, may be the manipulators, in this case, leading voters to believe that they will have a better life after the election. At the end of it all, people will realize that no changes have been made, and they will lose faith in the system.

People Are Being Treated Like Children

The media may regularly focus on manipulating the public.
When they continuously manipulate the public, it is an indication that they are treating people like children. The media will attempt to brainwash people by using sugarcoated arguments, intonations, and characters. In turn, the media will assume that people are immature and incapable of dealing with the truth. The primary goal is to ensure that the target audience is docile and submissive and that they react as expected. People are unable to think like adults as a result of media manipulation.

Using Emotions to Influence People

The media has learned more about how to manipulate people's emotions, and their main goal is to keep people from thinking critically. Various media outlets with agendas want to control people's thoughts. You should investigate how effective fear is as a tool.

Keeping the Public Ignorant and Mediocre

Some media organizations prefer to work with people who are uneducated and uneducated. The media can easily manipulate the public by isolating them from various pieces of knowledge; this is also true for certain politicians. Because people are ignorant, the media also ensures that a rebellion does not occur.

Encouraging the Public to Accept Substandard Performance

It is similar to ensuring that the general population is ignorant by ensuring that the public accepts mediocrity. When it comes to manipulating people, the media prefers to employ such tactics. Is the media, for example, airing the shows that people want to watch?

Is it true that some shows are imposed on us by the media? In short, do we get to consume the content we want, or does the media force us to consume different types of content? At times, it is clear that the media is brainwashing us, and we have lost interest in our surroundings. Furthermore, we have been socialized to be mediocre.

Self-Blame

The media frequently promotes self-blame and ignorance, as well as the belief that people are to blame for their misfortunes. In short, the media will focus on self-incrimination and will work hard to keep the public from mobilizing at all costs.

Completing the Public's Knowledge

The media has focused on learning more about its audience to gain more control over the general public. To easily manipulate the masses, the media can collaborate with other companies to learn more about each individual.

It is recommended that you learn more about how to detect media manipulation.

Because there are few resources discussing how to detect media manipulation, we are unable to delve into the topic in depth.

However, if you pay attention, you will notice when various media outlets are attempting to manipulate people.

CHAPTER 12
TRICKS FOR REALIZING YOU
ARE BEING MANIPULATED

How to Deal with People Manipulation

It may take some time to realize that someone is emotionally exploiting you. The signs are subtle and change over time. However, if you believe you are being treated in this manner, trust your instincts. Following that, there are some tricks we could employ to become aware that we are being manipulated:

Accept Apology for Your Role and Move On

You are unlikely to receive an apology, but you are also not required to dwell on it. Accept responsibility for what you believe you were doing and then say nothing about the other allegations.

You are not required to defeat them.

This game should not be played by two people. Instead, learn to recognize the techniques so that you can properly practise your responses.

Understand Your Basic Human Rights

The most important rule to remember when dealing with a psychologically manipulative person is to know your rights and recognize when they are violated. You have the right to self-defence until you endanger others. On the other hand, you may lose those rights if you cause harm to others.

Stay away from self-blame and personalization.

Because the manipulator's goal is to exploit your vulnerabilities, it is understandable that you may feel bad or even blame yourself for failing to satisfy the manipulator. It is critical to remember that you are not the problem in these situations; you have been manipulated to feel bad about yourself for you to give up your power and rights.

A "No" Is a Full Sentence

Learning the art of communication entails learning to say "no" diplomatically but firmly. It allows you to stand your ground while maintaining a relationship if articulated effectively. Remember that your basic human rights include the freedom to express yourself, the freedom to say "no" without feeling ashamed, and the freedom to live your own happy and healthy life.

Use Your Time to Your Advantage

Aside from unreasonable demands, the manipulator will frequently expect an immediate response from you to increase their power and influence over you in the situation. During these times, instead of reacting to the manipulator's appeal immediately, consider using the time to your advantage and distancing yourself from its immediate impact.

Consequences must be established.

If a psychological manipulator continues to push the boundaries and refuses to accept "no" for an answer, the outcome will be used.

The ability to identify and demonstrate consequence is one of the most important skills you can use to "stand up" to a stubborn person (s).

The outcome, expertly crafted, gives the deceptive person pause and compels them to shift from abuse to respect.

CHAPTER 13
CLOSING CHAPTER

Thank you for reading ***Dark Psychology and Manipulation***, I would like to invite you to the next book in this series (***Dark Psychology and Persuasion***).

The power of persuasion will be the focus of this book. Persuasion is nothing more than using one's mental abilities to form words and feelings to persuade others to do things they may or may not want to do.

Some people are better at persuading than others. And some people are easier to persuade than others.

The ease with which you can persuade others is directly related to their current mental or emotional state. Someone lonely or tired is easier to persuade because their defences are down. Someone in need may be easier to persuade than someone with a strong sense of self-worth.

People who are in a bad place in their lives are easy prey for those who try to persuade them to do something they would not normally do.

The concept of reciprocating is central to the first step in persuasion. When someone does something nice for someone else, the recipient usually feels obligated to do something nice in return.

If a neighbour assists an elderly neighbour with carrying groceries from the car, that neighbour may feel obligated to bake homemade cookies for that person. A coworker who contributes to the completion of a project is more likely to receive assistance when it is required. Many people constantly do nice things for others without expecting anything in return.

Someone to keep an eye on is someone who does nice things for others and then mentions some small favour that can be done in return.

Nonprofit organizations use this strategy to increase donations to their causes. They will frequently send a small trinket or gift to entice people to donate larger sums of money or even to donate where they might not have otherwise.

The idea is that the person opening the letter has received a small gift for no reason, so they may feel obligated to reciprocate.

Some people are naturally inclined to defer to authority. People in positions of authority can command blind respect simply by acting a certain way or wearing a uniform.

The problem with this is that authority figures, or those who appear to be authority figures, can cause some people to do things they would not normally do if a person in a position of authority had not asked. And it is not limited to those in uniform.

People who carry themselves or speak in a certain manner may give the impression that they are someone they are not.

To be considered a credible authority, someone or something must be well-known, and people must have faith in the person or organization. An expert is someone who knows everything there is to know about a subject and is more likely to be trusted than someone with limited knowledge of the subject. However, the information must also make sense to the people who are hearing it.

The authority figure loses credibility if there is no semblance of accuracy and intelligence. Even if a person is recognized as an expert, they will lack persuasive abilities if they are perceived as untrustworthy.

The worst aspect of persuasion power is that scarce or

difficult-to-obtain items are perceived to be far more valuable. Diamonds are valuable because they are both expensive and beautiful.

They wouldn't be as interesting if they were just pretty stones.

Consistent rewards are far less appealing than inconsistent rewards. If a cookie falls every time a person rings a bell, they are less likely to waste time ringing the bell because they know the cookie reward will always appear.

If, on the other hand, the cookie only appears on occasion, people will spend far more time ringing the bell in case this is the time the cookie will fall.

There are methods for increasing persuasion power. It, like any other trait, can be strengthened by implementing a few strategies and practising regularly.

In the game of life, persuasion is a powerful tool. Persuasive people understand their incredible power and how to use it effectively. They understand how to listen and truly hear what others have to say. They are very good at connecting with others, which makes them appear even more honest and friendly.

They give others the impression that they are knowledgeable and can provide a sense of satisfaction. They also know when to take a break and regroup. They are not obnoxious. They are convincing.

Did you know that your body speaks louder than your words?
Body language is constantly at work, whether you are aware of it or not.

If you want to master the art of persuasion, you must not only understand (and correctly read) body language but also learn to use it to make your point.

Body language consists of a combination of hand and facial gestures, posture, and overall appearance.

Using these to your advantage, you can get people to do what you want without them realizing you're controlling the outcome of the conversation.

www.ingramcontent.com/pod-product-compliance
Lightning Source LLC
LaVergne TN
LVHW010909200726
843507LV00002B/552